Darling, may I touch your pinkletink

Darling, may I touch your pinkletink

John B. Lee

First Edition

Hidden Brook Press
www.HiddenBrookPress.com
writers@HiddenBrookPress.com

Copyright © 2020 Hidden Brook Press
Copyright © 2020 John B. Lee

All rights for poems revert to the author. All rights for book, layout and design remain with Hidden Brook Press. No part of this book may be reproduced except by a reviewer who may quote brief passages in a review. The use of any part of this publication reproduced, transmitted in any form or by any means, electronic, mechanical, photocopied, recorded or otherwise stored in a retrieval system without prior written consent of the publisher is an infringement of the copyright law.

Darling, may I touch your pinkletink
John B. Lee

Cover Design – Richard M. Grove
Layout and Design – Richard M. Grove

Typeset in Garamond
Printed and bound in USA
Distributed in USA by Ingram,
       in Canada by Hidden Brook Distribution

Library and Archives Canada Cataloguing in Publication

Title: Darling, may I touch your pinkletink / John B. Lee.
Names: Lee, John B., 1951- author.
Description: Poems.
Identifiers: Canadiana 20200258591 | ISBN 9781989786055 (softcover)
Classification: LCC PS8573.E348 D37 2020 | DDC C811/.54—dc23

for the love of my life
Cathy Jeanne Lee nee Morden

"... how much better is thy love than wine! and the smell of thine ointments than all spices."
Song of Solomon Iv, x

"... She opens
 her legs showing him her great beauty,
 and smiles, a bow of lips
 seeming to tie together
 the ends of the earth."
"Last Gods," Galway Kinnell

"... I want
 to do with you what spring does with the cherry tree."
from Twenty Love Poems, Pablo Neruda

"Secrets have no place in the orchid boat of her
body and old pink brain beneath the willows."
"She Lays," Molly Peacock

"... *Deep in my sex, the*
  glittering threads are thrown outward and thrown outward
  the way the sea lifts up the whole edge of the body,
  the rim, the slit where once or twice in a lifetime
  you can look through and see the world —
  it is this world, without us,
  this earth and our bodies
  without us watching."

             "*A Woman in Heat Wiping Herself,*"
             Sharon Olds

"*Look, ... there he is.*
Now use your love arts. Strip off your robe
and lie there naked, with your legs apart.
Stir up his lust when he approaches,
touch him, excite him, take his breath
with your kisses, show him what a woman is."

           Gilgamesh, I, x

"There are little folds of skin all over the place; you can hardly find it. The little hole underneath is so terribly small that I simply cannot imagine how a man might get in there, let alone how a whole baby can get out! ... until I was 11 or 12, I didn't realize there was a second set of labia on the inside, since you couldn't see them. What's even funnier is that I thought urine came out of the clitoris. In the upper part, between the outer labia, there's a fold of skin that, on second thought, looks like a kind of blister. That's the clitoris."

           Anne Frank from the unexpurgated edition of
           The Diary of Anne Frank

If love be blind, love cannot hit the mark.
Now will he sit under a medlar tree
And wish his mistress were that kind of fruit
As maids call medlars when they laugh alone.—
                                Act II, i, Romeo and Juliet

"*On sizzling summer days*
we gathered in Hendrie's hen-
house and waited for Joanne
to lower her panties and expose
the hairless cleft between
her thighs and blush like a
ribald rose …"

                    lines from "Taboo," by Don Gutteridge

"… *I would love to kiss you.*
The price of kissing is your life.

Now my love is running toward my life shouting,
What a bargain, let's buy it."

                    lines from "A Great Wagon," by Rumi
                    translation by Coleman Barks

"The wave that died the death which lovers love,
Living in what it sought ..."

> lines from "The Boat on the Serchio,"
> by Percy Bysshe Shelley

"And pryvely he caughte hire by the queynte"

> from the Miller's Tale by Chaucer

"Lord God, Thou maketh Adam
and then maketh Eve to be his comfort.
From this coupling, all of Humanity
Has had descent.
Now I, sweet Lord, take my kinswoman,
Sarah as my bride;
So that we may mother children,
and deserve to live long a couple."

> From The Gospel of Tobit Viii,
> translation by George Elliott Clarke

Darling, May I Touch Your Pinkletink*

...and I am good and I am true and I believe, I do I do I do
as though just for a moment
I might travel back in time
for the child within the man is also me
I'm father to myself in this
I swear I'll keep him warm and love him well

> lines from my poem
> "Don't You Just Love a Christmas Parade"

---

* A pinkletink is a tiny frog whose song is a harbinger of the first arrival of spring.

i

The very first awareness of my own particular gender goes to only occasion I can recall bathing with my father. I was three years of age when we moved into the six-bedroom brick farmhouse. Prior to that we had lived in a small clapboard house with no indoor plumbing. My mother trained me on a potty chair in an upstairs bedroom, and my older sister and I took our ablutions in winter in a galvanized tub set upon water-soaked newspapers in the kitchen, or in summer out under the laundry line south of our dwelling. To relieve ourselves, we visited the two-hole outhouse under the pear tree in the orchard next to the shed. Our mutual nakedness was a matter of no particular concern to either of us. Perhaps I played *'what's this thing'* in the cradle, or *'what's this thing'* in the crib. That I don't recall, though I do remember my father and I sloshing about in the big bathtub in the brand new bathroom by the kitchen in the big house. And he teased me by drawing my attention to the little man bobbing between my legs like small soap, my circumcised prepuce emerging through the sudsy grey-water surface as though to take a breath like a long-necked one-nostril turtle come up for air. I confess it was a very innocent moment. But somehow I felt *shamed*. I'm a boy and you're a man. We share a common gender, he and I. My father the sire, and I his son and heir, the little prince of Leeland Farms, I was formed in his image. I stepped up and out of the tub and into the warm terrycloth embrace of my mother's towel, hot-water red, my new knowledge erect, and my eyes were opened and I knew that I was naked and beguiled.

ii

Every night for the longest while after we'd moved into the big house I slipped into my sister's bedroom for want of company. I was only three and still afraid to sleep alone. I did not understand why it mattered so much to my parents that I sleep in my own bed. After storybooks and nursery rhymes and bedtime prayer, "Now I lay me down to sleep," when my mother returned to the parlour, I'd slip out of my own crib and sneak into my sister's bed. She was two years my elder and we giggled and squirmed and fell asleep and then father or mother would come into the room and insist that I get back in my own bed where I belonged. I had no idea why it mattered. I suppose to them it was like separating the ewe lambs from the ram lambs or the bull calves from the heifer calves to be sure there'd be no life-early hanky panky. I'm only guessing. But to me it was a mystery beyond my ken. If we'd have been brothers, I suppose it might have been okay. As it is, I knew if I disobeyed I'd be spanked. I'd been warned. "Get in your own bed where you belong! Or else." Eventually I complied. Though it would be years before I would comprehend why.

iii

As my father would have said had he been there, we were *up to no good* ... four feral children running wild on the farm – two sons of Adam; two daughters of Eve – each of us in our abandon wishing to take the first bite of forbidden fruit. We were angels of innocence beguiled by the serpent and seeking a place to hide in the lost garden well away from the thistles and thorns of a disapproving gaze.

We sought in the fields and furrows, we sought in the high mows under roof beams and on the low-down granary floors, we sought in the shelter of cornrows with the froufrou of silks on the wind, and in the cow-crush of the pasture, in the dips and in the hollows of the land and in cribs and in sheds, in every lilac-fragrant shadow and the largess of split-leaf shade, in the tall grasses sweeping the orchards, by the fencerows and in the reeds of the pond where the dragonflies sang with gossamer wings and ultramarine bodies flung aloft and piercing the light in the wetlands and the woodlots, in the prick of pine needles beyond the well, and also in web drift redolent of leaf rot and grey mould, and also in dank earth damp in the cellar, and deep in the rich loam thick with the bursting of seed - and what we wanted – they with their warm little ruins like soft shells salt-moist from the sea, and we with our stones and small rods stiff to the root of the loins – what we wanted was to lie with our secrets between us and crushing together in naked confusion - like heat in the beast on the meadow, unlocking the thighs and crowning the stem with dark flesh in delight, to lean there and to know by adulation like roses blooming in rainfall and honeycombs drenching the hive.

And so after searching like strangers we arrived in a room. As we had planned we played a game of 'you first' and I who drew the short straw fell to disrobing. Just as I began to reveal what we'd all come for, the door scraped open and my mother came in with the laundry warm from the line. I stood there shamed to be caught and like original sin I hid myself as though from the eyes of God in fear because I was naked.

And my mother took me aside and said, "No shame. It's only natural to be curious. You must always remember to respect your body." And though I blushed to be schooled, I cherished her kindness forever. And I tell you this story in love and remembrance.

... they with their flesh like fruit spoil, like petals that bloom in the sun, we with out short staffs throbbing ... *and the smell of thine ointments ... and the spiced wine of the juice of ... pomegranate ... hands dropped with myrrh, and fingers with sweet smelling myrrh ...*

We humans — born naked in youthful sorrow and innocent learning. Forgetful of how it once was *lest to put forth a hand, and take also of the tree of life, and live for ever ...*

iv

My father only spoke to me about sex twice in my life. When I was coming of age he took me aside and gave me the following bit of advise. "Never treat a woman with disrespect. Never bring the police to my door. And *never* play poker with an undertaker." And that was my dad. That was his wisdom. Otherwise I was on my own. I was an innocent and I followed his advice to the letter. I never disrespected my mother, or sister, or cousins, or any of my female friends. I always treated every girl I knew with the utmost respect. I was a good and law-abiding citizen. And the opportunity to play poker with a mortician never presented itself.

Late in his life, he took me aside and confided that a nurse had asked him "Mr. Lee, how's your sex life?"

"Have you ever played pool with a rope," he replied.

"Oh Dad," I said. Like every child in the history of the universe, I did not want to know anything about my father's sex life.

V

I was recently breakfasting alone at the table of a local McDonalds waiting for my car to be repaired, eavesdropping on a conversation between a coffee klatch of elders. A cabal of septuagenarian gentlemen, co-conspirators conversing on the sex life of long-married humans.

"You still sleep with your wife?" one codger opined. "How the hell do you get any sleep? My old lady says I snore and she won't stay in the same room as me after the sun goes down. We don't even watch TV together any more. I go the basement and watch my sports, and she goes to the parlour and knits along with nothing much."

"Yep. I still sleep with her," the geezer replies. "We got a big bed. A bed so big she don't even know I'm there. It's a bed too big for both of us."

I smile and pretend I do not hear them as they drag chair legs squawking on the floor like schoolboys at the end of class.

I wonder what happens to lust in old age. I remember the Russian proverb, "old men talk of food and young men talk of sex." Now I'm in my sixties, I know that's not exactly true. What's true for me is this: sex still matters, albeit monogamous and loving sex within the sanctity of marriage. Sometimes it matters so much it makes its way into poems despite my best intentions. I've always been something of an innocent. Though perhaps I must confess that when puberty struck I would have had sex with a consenting knothole but for my commitment to the tenets I'd been raised by. I'd played the odd game of doctor and found that strangely exciting. But I remember my mother's caveat, her loving caution, "respect your body." So the poems in this collection are truth tellers. Like Shelley's line "the wave that died the death which lovers love," I know there's beauty in breaking the bonds of a private taboo. And so the poems herein contain something of what it was to be a child, something of what it was to be an adolescent, something of what it meant to be young and married and deeply in love, and something of what it continues to mean as I move, like a wave to the shore.

Yes, There is a Difference

Don and I
two aging poets
have come to consider
those curious *show me yours*
days of our youth
when we were engaged
in a game
we children called "playing doctor"

I remember
a cartoon on the wall
of the local garage
a pen-and-ink drawing
of a boy and a girl
each of them naked
but for their underpants
each of them
pulling the elastic waist band
wide open so the material yawed
like a big breath in the cotton
revealing a secret
as each looked down
at the other
in mutual amazement
the caption exclaiming

      "yes, there is a difference"

as though they hadn't otherwise known
in those early days of discovery
and fascination
the meaning of gender
manifest in genitalia

I being male
with my small self-knowledge
a cluster of three
gathered up in a cotton panel
a tailor's surmise, being
which side do you dress
in a trouser fly
something to guard
in a fight
or when unwanted lust
comes unintended
like a thumb poke in a pocket
puckering out when you walk

and what of the girls
oh, the girls
in their gussets
and heat panel panty hose
what of the girls
in their wind-lifted skirts
what of the girls
and the ache of first menses
what of the girls in the night
when in the long-before loving
foolhardy moonlight
when feathering makes them most shy
and what were we feeling
in blushes of strangest desire

our bodies
with thrills of regret
running through us

oh how we longed
to touch and be touched

I think of the pluck of an apple
of the loss
to the branch
as it leaps to the sky
in surrender
its shadow
a breath in the branches
no longer
the blossoms of spring
no longer the bee hold of April
its summer perfumes, then autumn
when it's wine in the grass
and November
the month I was born in
remembers me well
into winter and early-come darkness
the white on the ground
hiding all

Table of Contents

Darling, May I Touch Your Pinkletink (preface) – *p. xvi*

Yes, There is a Difference – *p. xxiii*

Childhood

– Anatomy Lesson – *p. 3*
– Seeking the Words for the Body – *p. 4*
– Becky Thatcher's Dream – *p. 5*
– Oh, how very, very sweet! How lovely! – *p. 6*
– If I Were Not Once Adam Dreaming in the Lonesome Garden of the Lord – *p. 7*
– Though I Sleep Fearless – *p. 8*
– Thinking Back – *p. 9*
– Proud – *p. 10*
– Overheard – *p. 12*
– Secret Desires – *p. 13*
– The Male Gaze – *p. 14*
– And Yet Though We Were Children – *p. 16*
– Sweet Linoleum – *p. 17*
– The Girl on the Wagon – *p. 19*
– Looking Down – *p. 20*
– Swimsuit Waltz – *p. 20*
– The Quiet Ones – *p. 22*
– The Luxury of Lust – *p. 24*

Adolescence

– Origin – *p. 29*
– The Body's Fool – *p. 30*
– And there was this – *p. 31*
– all short-skirt poems – a contemplation of Milton and Herrick in my teenage years – *p. 32*
– The Sun in the West Moving West – *p. 34*
– Silphium - the madness of love – *p. 35*
– Anne Frank's Vagina: a love poem – *p. 37*
– On Being a Teenager and seeing Lara after she's been ravished by the lawyer Victor Ippolitovich Komarovsky in David Lean's film Dr. Zhivago – *p. 39*
– L'Appelle du Vid – *p. 41*
– Look Over Your Shoulder and See Me – *p. 42*
– The Sin of Wishing – *p. 43*
– Everyone Does – *p. 44*
– Original Sin – *p. 46*
– Oh What a Very Different Time it Was – *p. 47*
– Voluptuous – *p. 48*
– The Lifeguard in Winter – *p. 51*
– Remembering the Present – *p. 52*

Youth

– My All and Only Purpose – *p. 57*
– A Great Weakening – *p. 58*
– Lifting the Leaf – *p. 60*
– Natural Acts – *p. 62*
– Dark Heart of my Memory – *p. 63*
– Okay, So There are Flowers ... – *p. 64*
– You Knew This Would Happen, Didn't You – *p. 66*
– Unlike myself in nether regions of myself I rarely see – *p. 68*
– and this ... – *p. 64*
– The Buffalo Bull at the Zoo – *p. 70*
– ... if we worry about love, why not war – *p. 71*
– Stone Horses – *p. 72*
– Darling, may I touch your pinkletink – *p. 73*
– Peeling Burn – *p. 75*
– The Leaf of Eve Becoming the World – *p. 76*
– In the Midst of My Sweet Confusion – *p. 77*
– ... on finding a volume called "The Feminine Orgasm" in amongst used books set out on a long table at a rummage sale in the vestry of Grace Anglican Church in Port Dover etc. ... – *p. 78*
– The Stone Woman – *p. 80*
– Victorious Virgin – *p. 82*

Old Age

– Make That My Metaphor – *p. 87*
– Were I – *p. 88*
– The Light that Sees Us – *p. 90*
– In the Muddy Bed of Creation – *p. 92*
– Bewilderment of the Heart – *p. 94*
– Open – *p. 95*
– My Love is Like an All-Day Rain – *p. 96*
– A Tourist in Bath Considers Lovers from the Past – *p. 98*
– Ode on the Lake as Lover – *p. 100*
– When Love is Like Knocking the Clay from the Plough – *p. 101*
– On Saying Farewell to a Mattress – *p. 103*
– Unseen – *p. 104*
– Syntribating Sweetheart – *p. 106*
– A Bed Too Big for Both of Us – *p. 107*
– Swept Away – *p. 109*
– Far Off in the Night Sky – *p. 112*

– If I Were So Compelled by Life – *p. 115*

An Essay/Review by Vanessa Shields – *p. 116*

Author Biographical Note – *p. 118*

Childhood

Anatomy Lesson

when I was seven
and you were six
I saw you racing past me
in your all together
your coral-coloured female body
fascinating to behold in lamp-lit soft relief
like the morbidezza
of a work of art
I confess
I was filled with awe
to glimpse a flash
of the incomparable beauty
of the fold of flesh
triangulated in the nether regions
contoured between your girlish thighs
so different from my own
cluster of three down there …

Seeking the Words for the Body

we were there together
in the two-gendered upstairs hallway
on the farm
out of earshot
of the adult world
when we were young
and body-wonderful children
curious to know
the most perfect word
for those private places
we dare not touch
even by saying aloud
forbidden words
we were tasting the sinful lexicon
of that devil's dictionary

look down and tell me
about beauty then ...

Becky Thatcher's Dream

as though she were slowly walking
ever deeper
into water rising as the bottom
silts away in shallow dips of sand
she lifts her linen hem
so the white reveals
itself in frills and flounces
where the dainty flower
of her maiden form
ruffles inward round
the gusset like a garland
from a dream
she's teasing Tom to madness
in his solitary night
inviting kisses
in the cotton
with a gentle trace of kissing
from within
and now the ghost of feeling
stirs the misty air
where vapour touches vapour
in a darkness
darker still …

Oh, how very, very sweet! How lovely!

did you dream of me
as I once dreamed of you
in the fragrant darkness
of a farmhouse night
tasting the fruit
of the knowing tree
where it lingered in wait
of the sentient hand
like the heart responding in the breast
of evening
oh to wind the fragile stem
to the breaking point
to feel it leap within the branch
that learns the loss in the shivering leaf
like the lifting away
of a bird in flight
that fluttering of absent wings
where the body
hosts all sleep
        eventual and perfect sleep

      and oh, how very, very sweet!
how lovely!

the bountiful and fertile beauty come alive
in the secret garden of our youth
where we might greet
the spirit of the Lord
walking in the cool of the day
like the moving shadow of first desire
that forms with the coming to life
within the self-astonished mind
as memory *is* the sensual twin of light ...

If I Were Not Once Adam Dreaming in the Lonesome Garden of the Lord

in the innocent libertinage
of my youth
when I dreamed a chimerical girl
with her six-thirty hands
telling time to the sensual clock
of her body in sleep
each palm
like a leaf of Eden
each cuticle moon
with its tide
in the pulse of the heart
blushing coral
on the liquefied shores of her darkening flesh

and I wonder as I dreamed
was she also not dreaming of me ...

saying *yes*
to her roseate flower

as though I were there
in the phantom of fingers

there in that trembling
shadow   sublime

Though Now I Sleep Fearless

when I was very young
and easing my limbs
in the sheets
like a sculpture unrevealed
or a half-completed ghost
set to the shape
of someone's beloved son
lying alone in the white float
like a bed-maker's child
I would
draw the covers up to the crown
blinding myself to dark corners
where old shadows menace
the safety of night
and what was it
haunting the coils but the creaking
dust demons of cold linoleum
breathing like the pulsing open
of midnight spiders burning with hunger
and who
might not fear
the heat in the house
roaring to be heard
for want in blue fire
and what then
of the wind in the casement
rattling occupied glass
like black ice shining over lost faces

how long the dream bringers waited
going heart slow
in the forelock
all those moon-timed evenings ago
stealing youth from this life
sleep by sleep

Thinking Back

Mostly what creeped me out
as a boy
was the unwanted attention
of certain old well-meaning women
doyens in Persian lamb coats
and fox tail tippets
cheap pearls and big-bosom broaches
closing in
with wet-mouthed kisses
wearing too much rouge and
red lipstick
leaving crimson scars smeared
on my forehead
like the lovelorn lips of a stranger
with a plastic jangle retreat
of dime-store bracelets
for music
and the oversweet lilac and lavender
fragrance lingering
like perfumed smoke in my nostrils
and oh *wasn't I cute*
wouldn't I someday
break all the girl's hearts

me with my tousle-haired cowlick
and big blue eyes
me with my peach-fuzz cheeks
and cowboy breeches
my homemade shirts
with the unmatched buttons

I wanted to say *keep your distance*
but wasn't I just their little man dandy
caught in the trap of embraces
with the snap of a hasp
for the proof of a tear in their purses

Proud

when I was a little boy and she was a little girl
she was body-proud and I was grateful
for the gift she gave
pulling her panties down
to reveal the lovely fold
of her maiden flower
easing her thighs wide
with pale flesh pressed close within
like the petals of a crushed corsage

and then lifting her hips to the light
in a showy fashion
seeming to say
see me there how lovely, oh how lovely
loving my vulva would be would be
oh how lovely loving my vulva would be

to feel someone touching me there
oh please do touch me there
caress me with your fingertips
trace my trembling with your fingertips

feel oh feel where the sweet cleft is gilded in pink
and ruffled within by labial silk and most intimate satins
set with the pip of its clitoral pearl
vermillion and pink and coral colour
scented by the fragrance
of vaginal flora and musky micturate
aromatic flavours stolen from the exotic spices
of the unknown swells of a far off sea
an ultra-exotic far-away tropical sea

you might lick the dews of liquefied flesh
you might lick if you wish
from the liquefied flesh
from the ultra-smooth liquefied flesh
for want of the tastes of the body
oh tasting the tastes of feminine body
there at the sacred font of the body to yearn
for the vinegar and the sweet fruit and the traces of salt
and the strangely metallic flavours of old coins washed in the sea

Overheard

Oh, what are they doing
I wonder, I wonder
Oh what are they doing I wonder
in there
as I listen outside the bedroom door
overhearing
the slightest slap sounds
oh I wonder

what's the sweet agony
of the three girls within
who seem to be suffering
in midday darkness
who seem as though
they must be spanking
each other for want of being bad
and I know that I'm a boy and am forbidden
to enter
even as a crack of light
beneath the door

oh there is something
going on in there, something
girls do beyond my knowing
a dishevelment
a devilment of sinning
as I hear the bedframe knocking the wall
like a blind in the wind
and then a crying out of mournful voices
falling into silence
I pretend to play in the hallway quiet
though I listen like a spy
holding my breath
hearing footfalls on the floor

Secret Desires

enduring long summers
of innocent water
we waded in the ultra-blue
soothe of the warm lake
where the cool creek of crescent beach
slipped like a clear school
of silver fry
shoaling through shallows
with a shivery caress
like a shadow
dragging its dark veil on the body
cupping the self in surrender
so on tiptoes
rising in the wave rock
of breakers by the sandy shore
to feel the intimate rhythms
of heaven's blooming
as it foamed at the heart then fell away
in the sizzle-sound of broken shells
and pebble-smooth green-and-blue bottle glass
what a lifting it was, what a buoyant
rocking from the instep
to the moon-white shoulders
then dizzying down in a swoon
to the fold of all secret desire
the flesh in its chrysalis
an unknown imago flexing invisible wings

The Male Gaze

what else might I do
but ogle the body before me
when we children
playing *school*
in the upstairs hall on the farm
were sent to the bedroom behind closed doors
to be punished by the teacher
and it was my room
and I the Wackford Squeers
of this particular day
awaited the necessary spank
with my twelve-inch measure
in hand
the wood slat calibrated by kings
and laced with an edge of steel
to keep the line straight
and true
to the graphite steady of hand
and sharp and to the point
as though
you might stab the page
with your pencil
cruel carpenter
of crude arithmetic
but we were pretending
an adult world
where every wrong
every imaginary conceivable wrong
might lead to this

a bettering

as though only by the rod and by the staff
and by the hickory stick swishing on flesh
we saw ourselves *stung*
as by red welts *improved*
so there we were
at seven and seeing
the pedagogical WACK!
as unavoidable truth
but I remember the awe
I felt
as panties dropped to the floor
and drooped at the ankles
with the white stumble of soft cotton
and the bent over body before me
and what I saw then
in the line of light
what thrilled me to the very root
stopped my ruler
and stayed my hand
as a mind might stray beyond measure
in a beautiful loop de loop
like a string come loose in blue wind

And Yet Though We Were Children
after a poem by Don Gutteridge

born to be mammal curious
we boys ached to gaze upon girls
with their lovely involutions
kissing soft cotton
like May lilies blooming in fabric

and what to compare
with the pursy show
of Ontario orchids dusted with light
hiding themselves in the shadow of trails
shy lady slippers and moonlit roses
concealing their secrets
crushing dream petals in the darkness of gardens

and what of the shore wash of moonlight
and lake shells
in the show me – oh –
show me the crests of desiring youth
to follow the slopes of the blushing
illusions of Eden to find there
the keeper of silence

that apple of knowledge
we lived to be knowing
with wind-fallen flavours
and the cider-rich fragrance of longing
what's spring in the bud's primavera
is lovely withholding
of winter its warning
a broken-branch wisdom
still falling

Sweet Linoleum

there on the cool earth
in the dog shade of the shrubbery
we children went
to reveal
the mystery of gender
one to the other
long before falling into shyness
in those show-me-yours years
when with an excited glance
we boys first glimpsed
what it meant to be seemingly bereft
though strangely beautiful
folding-in on nothing
or little girls were filled with wonder
to see the secret
that can't be kept
as with minor amazement
life lifted out of the nest
as fledglings show hunger in spring
and yet
we turned away
from cowboy kisses
we hid our faces in our sleeves
when the backdrop hero
fell from grace
by taking the starlet
in his leather arms
his glove gauntlets brushing the bonnet aside
for the trail's-end romance
that thankfully faded to black ...

Oh Robin Hood, surely Maid Marion wants
an arrow in the sheriff's breast
an arrow
singing death to wrong
in the evil throng that roils beyond the parapet
not Eros finding his home in her damsel's heart
the shaft of desire quivering like a reed
in agitated water

Oh Superman
bespectacled at your desk
or rushing through blue sky
above the city
your cape shivering like a banner in flight
over Metropolis
your leotard turning to stone
we were grateful
for the distance you maintained
with that grey-suit gormlessly shrugging one shoulder
impervious to Lois Lane's schoolgirl crush
how discomfiting all desire
seemed like Kryptonite to the office boy in you

however curious
we were
beneath the bed in ghost light
lying among the dust gather
that feathered the hip
what clung to our clothing
like delicate seed kites
from crossing dark meadows
into the deep grass far from imaginary fences
gave memory a soft grey monument
and dream its hint of the cosmos
and night
its sweet linoleum

The Girl on the Wagon

one hot day
in a sun-golden field of our youth
we were all there for the harvest
riding ruts over uneven ground
with one girl daring the sway
of the rack on the wagon
as she climbed to the sky that was shining
like steel burned blue by the heat

and she risked the last rung
rising through perils
above the jog of the tongue
and clevis
when the draw bolt
rang in its lock
then she suddenly slipped
at the shock as we stopped

but the hired man reaching up
with his work-blackened palm
kept her from falling

the rumour of his lifeline
branding her thigh

like angels ashamed to be good

Looking Down

Before knowledge broke her body open
looking down
at the lovely declivity
between her thighs
what did she think
of the sweet nothing, the cleft
over which
she first crossed herself
in modesty
fanning her palms
as young girls do in photographs
gripping one finger
in innocent decorum
holding her hands there, then
seeking one leaf for an apron
hiding herself where she dimples inward
like a blink in the flesh
the hint of her fertile fold
like a breath taken in before wishing

oh, once they were both
rain-loved children of Eden
she like a rose in the glade and he
like asparagus spearing the sky
when there at the dawn of creation
with God in the garden of morning
they hid from his numinous glory

two shadows caressed by the light
secret thoughts caught by meaning in flight

The Swimsuit Waltz

> "... and the eyes of them both were opened
> and they knew they were naked ..."
> Genesis III, vii

when I was young I watched the girls
to see the fold within the soft reveal
of water rising
as they waded
into waves to wet the slightly dimpled
gusset licked by gentle crests
that rose to greet the cloth
enhancing colour so caressed
as though the bay had brushed the fabric
like an artist's brush
dipped in the shining paint
to make a blushing stroke
of deepening shade
pearled by exhausted light with light's
involvement there
both girl and water in romance
tiptoe waltzing to and fro and up and down
to mark the cool surrender
of the heart-warmed flesh

The Quiet Ones

if I were young again
and playing
the innocent game
of *show me yours*
in the orchard grass
and the corn rows
in the gentle light
of gloaming
with summer swarming
the treetops
slow burning with shadowy angel-winged midges
those short-life choirs
weaving and waving
like gossamer fabric
snagged by the breeze
on the delicate tips of high branches

what did I make
of the beauty revealed
by the secret confusion of sex
where it enters the delicate fold
like the favours of Eden
snapping their stems
when the leaf comes away with the fruit

what might I do or have done
with the knowledge I'd gained
from the watching of horses
or hearing the herd bull
bellowing darkness
hollowing over the door
who but a farmer's son
chalking the rams

or counting the lambs
in the spring
with his father's arm hot to the wrist
in a breach
while the feline is purring and rubbing her hip
on a feedbag
and the heifer
is standing her ground

The Luxury of Lust
after a line in a poem by Don Gutteridge

what might I learn about girls
as a boy on the farm
watching heifers
in first heat on the meadow
with young bulls
in the bull yard bellowing
testing the fence with their shoulders
the old fellow *Cloudburst*
father of calves
raising his head to the door
and pawing the straw in his pen
with much on his mind
though these were his daughters
their scent on the wind
like urine on flowers
he's mad
in barn shadows
they're too young to be bred
though they're strange with desire
and mounting the cows
as they graze
it would be death to their growing
as yearlings
small mothers small calves
born hard
like those who must live
a stupid life
giving over to unfamiliar urgencies
of the flesh
I think back on grade nine girls
in white go-go boots and
red miniskirts tugged tight
and crossing their thighs on wonder

what comingling confusion
of love and concupiscence
pheromones clinging
to the small thatch
like beads of dew
to the thread-thin stems of the grasses
of dawn

mine - like Romeo's ruined mind
remembering the truth in the body
and being young
… I'm grateful now
for the slow surrender
of wise caution
though I know by starlight
and melons
I know by milk shine and green weed
by broad leaf
and its shadow
by the sorrow of corn
pale in wet land
how artless and awful
the seed and the soil
in the moonlight or morning
the moon like a barn stone hung in blue heaven
what the tomcats were crooning
was *warning*

Adolescence

Origin

"And pryvely he caughte hire by the queynte"
from the Miller's Tale by Chaucer

imagine God's great finger
sculpting Eve
shaping her there
in the malleable mud
of her beautiful body
tracing her breasts and
forming the labial petals
and pink throat
of her flower
setting the pearl of pleasure
at the coral-coloured threshold
within the silken crowning of flesh
spicing desire with fragrant pheromones
and sacred ointments
from deep within the seed chamber
of her feminine fold
awaking to a first coupling
life enclosed in her vulvar circumference
the globe of fruit in her hand
its flavours of sinning on her tongue
her mind flooding with knowledge
like bees and sparrows
and all the living denizens of her wilderness garden
as she has opened
to receive her lover
feeling the surging glories
in voluptuous waves of creation
under the star-milting moon-milken sky
finding joy in a kiss divine
among rain-struck roses
and wings taking flight from the sea

The Body's Fool

at the end of summer's day
after playing scrub in the farmyard for hours on end
with me the only boy in an innocent game of girls
she clicked the handheld torch and focused the flashlight's beam
so it shone like an evening moon
encircling the small darkness
of her heart-warmed denim fold
as though from the seam of a chrysalis
it were importuning the sweet mystery of her vulva
pressing the stitches
from within the blue weave like the energy of wings
on a lovely imago straining to be born

And there was this

casual lapse in decorum
as her skirt hem drifted high
along the sweet reveal
of her upper thigh
so I might glimpse
the double cloth
of her cotton gusset
with its hint of flesh
where the crease of her sex
impressed the fabric
in shadow fold
like the seam of a chrysalis newly formed
and she was farouche
a wild immodest creature
careless of the gentle line
of her maidenly paradise
touched there by the light
the intimate flesh of her gender
teasing in layers like a lily about to bloom
in a primavera garden
on a sunlit summer morning
a silken secret I longed to know
with my tongue, my eyes
my nose, my hand, to taste
to see to scent to feel
to savour the fragrance
like a scent of a mollusk rolling in from the sea
the colour of flesh, the flavour of musk
like cider and salt the texture of watered clay
and human heat and satiny damp
of that enclosure and depth
for all possible explorations of intimate flesh
in the pleasure petals of her inner sex
surrendering all as one might a flower
and she opened her thighs
to the centre of divine desire
as though in the book of the world
she flexed her ruffled pages
and I read

all short-skirt poems – a contemplation of Milton and Herrick in my teenage years

...then wilt thou not be loath
To leave this Paradise, but shalt possess
A paradise within ...
                John Milton Paradise Lost, Book XII, lines 585-588

this is for
all the short-skirt poems
of my innocent youth
for girls in culottes
and milk-white go-go boots
for those in louche socks
falling as they walk
and oh a lad thinks also in memory of
the hot-pant teens he's known
with an in-fold
blinking of the seam
or tight jean cutoffs
ragging at the tan line
with a threadbare blue

for the paper-white swimsuit
clinging to the warm flesh
next the goose-pimple lake
in the wash of water
where waves weep
as they rise and fall
with a cool greeting
like tongues that delight
in the tasting of sugar and of salt
oh for those areolas
blushing the cloth from within
like a ripening of berries

and to seek and find
in the swish and sway
of a hem's sashay
what the warm wind wants
of cotton zephyr's modesty is there
like Easter on the altars of the spring
or orchids in full splendor
of the sun

oh for me it was
a time of Julia and Juliet

it was an hour for the contemplation
of the apple flavoured sins of Eve

the vexing knowledge of her fig leaf's bliss
withheld
like smooth-fleshed fruit

with such an Eden in me
where the garden stirs in sleep
to reveal the blameless rose
abloom in moonlit bowers
its crimson petals
drinking dew

and so I too possess a paradise
within …

The Sun in the West Moving West

behind the accordion doors
of my uncle's house
in various degrees
of dishabille the girls and the boys
in separate rooms disrobe
within an intimacy
of lamp-lit shadows
that movement of clothing
caressing the boards
in varieties of disarray
like late spring lawns
under the fallen petals of magnolia
dropping in fragrant
discontinuity
to the river cottage floor
the flowering fabric of youth
in cottonwood whites
and seed-kite drifts
of the sweet breath of June
cascading through changes
like water receiving the wind at the shore
and then in rayon array
our great aunt
leading us down to the dock
like a duck mother
crossing the road to the ladder
as we lower ourselves
into life past the fragrance of gravel
and tar
dipping our bodies
each season anew
annealing the mutable muscles and curves
like young gods
you might dip to the heel
or the angel-form places
where sadness resides
with the sun in the west
moving west

Silphium – the madness of love

at the casual easing open of her knees
in recumbence on my bed
what might my young mind have done
but follow the soft line
of a shadow's caress
tracing a thought from
along the long bones
to where dimpled cotton
blinked into a crease at the white fulcrum
of her body
my attention fixed
there as though upon the closed calyx and incurving petals
of a late-spring lily
and she lying back
in skirt-drift indifference seemingly feeling carefree
and careless of the sensuous reveal
where the blue-veined thighs
presented their most superlative secret
as though in fragrant wonder
like an aromatic plum ripening in heat
and so in my youth
if I dreamed of that honey-chamber
lost in a locked garden
with forbidden hands
I dared not reach out to touch the delicate bloom
as though it were made from the burning stone
of a sculpture in the stone-scalding sun

and I am here now
where memory keeps the madness
of young love and lust alive as though folded
forever at the centre of desire in design
as I call upon
all the extinct silphium of ancient Rome
to be my ephemeral witness
by ghostly seed and spectral flower
by phantom fruit and insubstantial stem
and by the silver emblem of my human heart
even as far as the last and forever-innocent morning
with its three-lobed promise of green leaf shadow
awaiting the hand of Eve hiding her beauty
in the bowers of Eden

Anne Frank's Vagina: a love poem

There are little folds of skin all over the place; you can hardly find it. The little hole underneath is so terribly small that I simply can't imagine how a man can get in there, let alone how a whole baby can get out! ... until I was 11 or 12, I didn't realize there was a second set of labia on the inside, since you couldn't see them. What's even funnier is that I thought urine came out of the clitoris. In the upper part, between the outer labia, there's a fold of skin that, on second thought, looks like a kind of blister. That's the clitoris.

Anne Frank from the unexpurgated edition of
The Diary of Anne Frank

translate your body for me into love
like some exotic language
from the East
some ancient tongue I do not speak
long lost in time
the scrip in secret depths
scrimshawed beneath the drift of sand
to say what lies between the sway of spine
and loft of mind
to seek and find the natural lordosis
of this dancer's hand
so partnered
like the button count
upon a gently-fastened dress
or water's level in a carried vase
the shift of liquid volume
tips its slow meniscus in a sacred light
the shining dark and blue interior
of antique words contain
archaic vowels come in veils of breath and song
the sounds that hide
all secret meanings
in the deepest hour of the shadow dark
to bloom
as lilies do imagining the sun

to ripen
as the high peach swells
in shelter of its leaf-green warm
I come
to share the revelation of the stem
and step below in altitude beyond the shade
my reaching hand though blind is blind enough
to see it all
and in the seeing show ...

come taste the lexicon of life
and soon you will forget
the child though born
must die
but when we weep
our common tears must speak
as spirits do
in absent sounds that vanish in the wind

On Being a Teenager and seeing Lara after she's been ravished by the lawyer Victor Ippolitovich Komarovsky in David Lean's film Dr. Zhivago

What's Lara's beauty
have to do with consequence of love, I wondered
left as I was in adolescent contemplation
of her maiden-fold

her lovely face
so blushed and fevered by
the rushing of her quickening heart
she'd only come to crisis
in the tragic scene before

as I am there imagining a silken-petal rose
pulsing in a dark dishevelment
ravished by an agony of rain

she's ruined
by the very regions of her deepest want in storm
and story … a sweet surrendering
of the aching areola soaking inward like a berry stain
upon the flesh

the lip edge of her fervent flower
washed vermillion like a fragrant kiss
and I am lost
in that silken ruck of her ruby sheets
and open thighs
like curtains drunk with watered light

what then of her fatigue
her lazing knee
her ankle in its lassitude
all life is loss, I fear
… and shame

the apple's aftertaste
its knowledge also in the bud
and bitterly
blemished by the winding stem
the ripened drop
the bruise and pip

each holds some future shadow
for the leaf shade of tomorrow's sun

I'm there and cooling
like the heart gone still
that busy heart has fallen into sleep

and Lara's come to the parlour
with a pistol in her hand

L'Appelle du Vid

if in an early adolescent sleep
I dreamed a dream
a waking metamorphosis
wherein my maleness
like a chrysalis new shed
transformed itself
into a beautiful imago
emerging from the pupa bursting forth
as though new flowering
with delicate wings like watered silk
reshaping in the hands of some mischievous divinity of night
my inner belly plump with seed as though it were a pomegranate
ripening withal and there between the languorous bones dropped wide
I found a secret pearl concealed within a dainty shell
a jeweled vermilion pip set into its oyster-fragrant fold
a lovely involution to be by pleasure rubbed to pungent ecstasy wrung slow
what might I comprehend upon my swirling fingertips
by scent and deep caress
to press against my nose the meaning of the musky odor
of myself as new as though I'd found a lotus blooming
in a moonlit pond
its pulsing petals forming fondly on my cuticle moons
pushed in to fill the labial folds of liquefying flesh
to feel there a sweet circumference
as ultra smooth and satiny enough to please the mind
within a garden there between the thighs
the sweet sensorium
in alteration out of reach ...
no portion of experience
will suffice to name or understand
in lexicons beyond my ken and unavailable
to my design or my desire's delight
though I am quite content as half complete
to taste the knowledge of the tree of man
and graft that change to what remains the same
the naked under-leaf of Eden's fig upon the tongue of Eve
a word to speak and say the anima and animus
the inner leaving and the outer coming home
experience beyond the body's only form

Look Over Your Shoulder and See Me

my cousin and I
were silly boys
as we walked through the fairground midway
our arms bent
like short-winged birds
intent upon feeling
the brushing by of breasts
in the tight-packed crowd
of city girls
we let our minds
flow through the flesh
to the tip of the hair on the back of our hands
as though we might feel
the sweet rush
of an intimate rub
like a breeze over green on a leaf above berries
as angel intrusion
imagine a nipple's caress
that might leave a mark on the arm
like a beautiful bruise
what foolishness follows in youth
we gathered our knowledge of girls
like cockleburs and berry stains
or the dripping of wax where it cools
and we imagined that cupid stung through us
like a spy with a dart in his sleeve
with much late-at-night dreaming to follow
like faces at windows
and hands upon latches
unlocking desire
where it turns like a hip in hot sand
it seems a hundred years since then
… we're both old married men
so when my mother said
"what's the big deal about breasts"
I might have told her the story
of her barely adolescent son
in flight through the midway at midnight
saying 'you must look over your shoulder to see me
with the wings of a boy from the past'

The Sin of Wishing

all those years ago
when I was young
and a certain girl
sat on my bed
the two of us engaged
in the tease of adolescent conversation
our bodies strangely changing
as though the breath of God
were there within us
growing and feathering
with follicular whispers in new places
and she seemed indifferent to decorum
her plaid skirt
rucking up her thigh
the fine blond hair of her flesh
pricked up in goose bumps
and the immodesty of her
white cotton gusset
dimpled inward on the secret fold
where despite myself
I could not help but focus my attention
dreaming of what she barely concealed
and longing to reach across the counterpane
to trace the unseen fuse
of her perineum lacing the skin
from the pucker of her bottom
to the silken cleft of her flower
my own tumescent self crushing
against cloth and seam
I grew suddenly shy
and the moment passed
as she closed the big book of her thighs
saving us both from the glorious fire of paradise
as she stood and walked away
the hem of her skirt swaying like bell shadow
sounding the valley of temptation
with the perilous pleasures of iniquity

Everyone Does

... in a recent story appearing in the papers Paul McCartney confessed that he and John Lennon used to masturbate together crying out the names of famous women as they ejaculated

we are living in very different times
neither better nor worse, but strange
though when I was a boy
come of age
I thought that I alone
would lie
sinning in the shamefulness
of night
seeding the sheets in the dark
my most solitary mind fixed
upon the coupling place
that sea-fragrant locus
a fold concealed in white like a bandit's kiss
between the thighs
of every girl I knew
feeling that
deep in the root
masculine thrill
of coming to a crisis
of my own creation
like brilliant star swirl
of rural midnight heavens
locked in the loving enclosure
of natural dream
with the heat of the flesh
apparition a crowning companion
a chimera, weightless and insubstantial
as a veil of air
though my thoughts
made it real
as desire comes true
in the taste of a peach or

the touch of dragged silk
or the satin caress of still water
lit white by the moon
on the bay
warm wading I go
in the phantom of summer
or healing the frost
on the glaze of a pane
with the palm of my hand giving life
to the glass

what proved me a fool
like a shadow wind-loose in a garden
was the intimate pearl
like a jewel made divine
the gem that quickens the heart
like a hoof in a hill
or a wave crashing home on a stone
for we
are all a confluence
of rivers of life
flowing deep in the earth
or deep on the land
invisible visible we're all rivers the same
and the same

Original Sin

one summer
after sundown at the fairgrounds
we lay secreted
on the grassy gloaming
a conspiracy of children spying
with our bellies to the earth
and our hands upon our chins
watching the assignation
from a distance and what we saw in that blur
two half-naked bodies bucking
like beasts of the field
a boy and a girl
in flagrante dilecto
gone away the golden halo
gone as well the fanciful dream
and we knew her by name
this lost one
how strange to see her there
locked in this seemingly shameful embrace
both of them crying out in concatenation
for the pleasure they found there
where they were joined in coupling

our own particular demons
smouldering within
like an ancient fire
lit long ago
when lightning struck
the water
and first life crawled ashore

Oh What a Very Different Time it Was

In high school
we had an English teacher
who often teased
one particular female student
and though he seemed slightly fey
with fluttering eyelashes
and delicate hands and slender arms
of a girl
he grew a red beard
so he came to resemble
D.H. Lawrence the consumptive poet
whose novels and stories and poems we'd read aloud in class
Sons and Lovers, "The Rocking Horse Winner," "The Snake"
and we also knew about
the sexual fire
between the randy gamekeeper
and Constance Chatterley
we'd thumbed the burning fiction
of that forbidden book
in hidden places
and were familiar
with the ink-smudged dog-eared pages
and so we were
titillated by the banter
between this teacher
and his seemingly receptive student
trading bon mots
with whisperings
like the lacing of forget-me-nots
in secret places
with a trace of fragrance
a snap of flame
and the strange denouement
lingering between them

Voluptuous

when I think of the word *voluptuous*
I remember how once you longed to show me
where intimate flesh is made most pale
by sunlight leaving its summer line
along the whiteness of your inner thighs
and you are formed in labial flounces
like a four-petal rose
as though beneath the leaf of Eve
where garments hide
all present secrets of the flesh
infolding like the involutions
of a soft-shelled creature stolen from the sea
a fragrant and lubricious place
so scented with aromatic maidenhood
like wisdom lost
within the savoring of paradise
let me trace the body's knowledge
like the shaping of creation
in the garden where I dream

let me taste the sweet elixir of desire
as from the flesh of over-ripened fruit

my eyes behold vermillion
and my hands
caress a pearl in cradling silk

what laves the finger makes it keen
to feel the heat

I'll be your lover
like a lake wave rising as you wade

I'll craft a tide of senses
like the moon

oh voluptuous and fertile womb
the heart's companion
and life's sacred theme is there

while I sing
the crimson anthem of this breathing prayer
coloratura to the perfect darkness
of the inmost motions of the mind
I find the font of beauty in this faith of palms

oh let me change the past in this communion
to belief - the serpent in the starlight
fails his task and I am thus renewed
to become all innocence
and so
eternal in the monumental moment
of your manifest embrace

The Lifeguard in Winter

when the civic pool is drained
and grey
as a winter vault
and the air is silver
and the earth is white
and the cold
that creatures the land
of dead December
is laced with sleeping snakes
looped in ice like hawsers
in the frozen harbours
of the lake
I am reminded
of the sun-brown girl
seated in her summer throne
high above
the laughing water
a guardian angel
of deep-end dangers
her whistle like a bird throat
warning wild children
against the slippery perils
of wet cement
and watching
for the deep-end thrashers
in the blue fathoms
gulping and going down
twice too often and closing their chlorinated eyes
as though they might be holding their breath
for the want of a kiss divine
and I see now
how her season is done
how her image then
is laved in frost
where she shivers away
like wind-stirred smoke
and cannot hold for she

is fracturing along the crack lines
of her beauty
like a statue candied in ice

thus it is with time
when time
is tired of us all
and steals our living youth
and we grow old and older still

how might she whistle then
to warn herself
against the boreal dangers
of this frozen dream
when we are falling through
a thin-ice sky
and are tumbling upward
ever further into starlight
everything we touch then out of reach

Remembering the Present

my wife and lifelong lover
you confess of a callow foolishness
when you were a sexy schoolgirl
you say how you walked
barelegged for fashion all winter
down Wilson Ave
along the breakwall
above the slush-whitened flow
of the city river
as you went crossing the bridge
spanning the Thames striding up Dundas to Richmond
you walked past the old courthouse
where the ghosts of the hanged
linger in the mind of time
like grey fog strung out
in imaginary light
long past their time for fading
and it was
a cold wind teasing
your hem
like a nun's cruel measure
turning the flesh crimson
with a moral chill of immodesty
burning the flesh
like ice in fire
and there
like sleet-dampened paper
the morning's thin glaze
melting from glass
you arrived in your classroom
your bare flesh blushing with chill
and I wonder
at the warmth of true wisdom
like schoolbooks set open on the ink dry of lessons
and my own true learning becomes the memory of the shadow float
of the outline of your body falling even as darkness settles on snow

Youth

My All and Only Purpose

how erotic it remains to me my lovely wife
to briefly glimpse the wink of cloth
between your thighs
much like the crease line of a chrysalis

to see you stepping in the spa
to wish
the half-moon of my fingernail
to trace that dimpled tuck of cloth

to find and feel the warm enfoldment
of your feminary flower there

the rayon inlay blinks
to clothe a cleft in this reveal

and so I long to seek the fold
to kiss the double petals of your vulva's deep design

to taste the acrid nectar
from the sweet imago of those labial wings

all memory of loving set aside
to make a rediscovering

A Great Weakening

in my thoughts
I go back through time
as though
through the semipermeable
membrane
of an otherwise impassible moment
with the sand
rising in the wasp-waist
of a topsy-turvy glass
all cone
and dimple
of an upgathering
like the swirling skyward
of dust
in a wind-caught corner

and what of regret
what of joy or sorrow
who then
might be forgetful
of first things forgiven
when like seeds in earth
awaiting the deep soak
of come-to summer rain
we were breaking open
and green worthy
from the pip and the drupe
and the pearl in its shell
to the stone in the ripening peach
see how the wild
and the pampered
comingle in the thick confusion
of a life swollen ditch
or the fence at the edge of the field

how the mind enthused by sweet cane
might weaken
like watered clay
and in that subsidence
burst forth singing
as we do
when knowing makes the body shine

Lifting the Leaf

by the waters of the fourth river of Eden
and by the slumbering rib
and by the fruit
of the sinning tree
I confess me
of wanting a lexicon
in a language so lovely
it might make solemn
and sacred
the divine locus
of all human creation
set there in leaf shadow
that silken fold
of my young imagining
seen only then
in the soft reveal
of white fancy
and by the sweet permission
glimpsing the shy flower
I dare not name
a rare orchid of such beauty
blooming in moonlight
bone of my bone, flesh
of my flesh
let me gaze upon that garden
in the cool of the day
let me see
with open eye
what beguiled
the first bruise-heeled man
let me caress
and taste and savour
the fragrant vessel
the living font
from whence God shaped
with the midnight motion of his
moving hand a cleaving place

then set pleasure
as in its open shell
designed for deep responding
like a pebble in the brilliant liquors of a well

what shall I call this then
this seeking
in memory when time
might trace desire to its source
and there to find
the mutual illusion of a sword of fire
what shall we tell
the child within
the watered dust of us
go wake tomorrow's ghost
go wake the unborn eidolon
go wake the seed-pierced ovum
of the soul
then say
the shark is older
than the knowing tree
and from the molten shores
of flowing rock
from far beneath a mile of ice
lain heavy on the undulating lake
that lifts its voice in waves
then call the heaven blue
her black horizons closed by night
I'm there and gone
and gone and there again

in this I call my love to bed
where we recite
our loving
heart to heart
and hand to hand

Natural Acts

from when the sacred beauty of our mutable bodies
first began the sweet featherings of change
we were helpless to hold ourselves still
with the surreal awakening in the dream-clock of the flesh
each heart in the breast under bone
like a peach on a branch in the sun
with summers to swell in the heat
in the leaf-shadowed centre of every design
God's hand like a sculptor
moved shaping desire
as in fragrance we fall
to the earth
how then is it sinning to learn
the jubilant lessons of love

Dark Heart of my Memory

imagine my tongue
like a drone in a rose
or my breath
like the summer at rest
in the folding of wings
oh imago of light come close
as colour comes close
in the fragrance of words
dark heart
of my memory
what's savouring then
but unseen
as it is when the poets who dream
think of life in their youth
so cradle this mind
in your hands my love
like you're turning a gourd
in a garden
while midnight
is crowning the moon
with her brilliant tiara of stars
the amber corona of luminous mist in the sky
and winter comes climbing the shores
of the lake too soon
with undulous acres of ice
building a cumulous berm on the sand

to this season of bodies
I'm old
as the springtime's grown old
in the calendar since I was born

Okay, So There are Flowers ...

okay, so there are flowers
I might employ
in compare
lest the look of a lily in spring
closed up on its seam when it's pink in the green
be too close to be true
or the blooming Ontario orchid
alone on the floor of the forest
in a shadowy intimate darkness
of delicate things
the voluptuous purse of its petals
withholding itself in cool heat
near the fungus aromas
of trees in the morning
when light at its least
comes burning through shade
to burnish the silken corona
like the easing of hands on a lock
or a shell
yes, I call upon shells
to emerge from the sea
where the salt winds have left them
at the edge of the shore
what softening Venus
reveals to the life of a wave held within
don't mention the peril of pearls
in shelters of flesh
to the secret release of a quickening heart
we are creatures of flavour as well
seeking acrid elixirs
like cider from apples and oils
of Gethsemani seeping through stone

and what of this hand
in the night
change the water for roses
see their liquefied thirst in a mutable ruff
how lovely each moment
each movement each touch
like the blushing of brushes
lifting colour from tears

You Knew this would happen, Didn't You

all those years ago
sitting at the Ceeps hotel
amongst the mostly jolly jocks
drinking dime draft
in the stale-wet beer smells
and the glassy aromas
of smoky light
midst the chemical stink
of burning words
and half-heard conversations
drowned out and shouting
with trays full of empties
carried across the room
on the upraised arm of the waitresses
like clinking sombreros
flung high and drifting with the weird glamour
clouded by suds
and the empty sorrows
of misspent time
how the mind wondered
in its youth and promise
what might yet come
what unseen faces
and unmet strangers
waited in life
with Shakespeare dead
four-hundred years
and the snap of fire in seed
with an intaken breath
that glows in the drooping ash
what it is to look now
back upon the boy
you were

the one who once sat
imagining the man
he might become
with someone else
grieving the mystery
when the sun comes up on *nothing*
while the moment of greatest amazement
awaits him
in the fool's skull of tomorrow

Unlike myself in nether regions of myself I rarely see

oh how I long to feel the secret garden in the flesh
the love that eases open like a wound divine
where sacred energy begins in female beauty
with its quick and frantic swim

desire redolent deep and wonderful
and fragrant as a labial shell
that lies upon the shore
beside an ever liquefying tide

how unlike myself
in nether regions of the self
I rarely see

to contemplate that sweet encompassment
with silken flounces like the petals
of a rose in bloom

while creation surges
inward wave on wave
as pleasure thrills to hold
the root within the fertile earth

the all-embracing soil contends
to feel the sensual pull and swell
and counter-swell
of growth in motion

seeking rain in rivers
caverns deep where the water seeps
and soaks the softening stone
and vanishing sky

in warm involvement
with the darkness well beyond the light

and this …

remove the leaf my love
where knowledge makes you shy
and I will
be the shade beneath
the restless shadow
of a walking eye
to call it sin
improves on darkness
darker still within
the moon-fold
of a silent kiss
the hurry-hearted sigh
one silver tear to cry

and this …

The Buffalo Bull at the Zoo

the bison bull
his nose peeled back
in a nostril snuffle
taking a deep inbreath
of the pheromones of the cow in heat
his great erection
unsheathing
like a sword from silk

he stands in the amber wash
of her desire
discerning the scents of estrus
like an expert perfumer
he's teasing apart the multiple notes
of the fragrance of the womb
from the odors of her urine
dripping on the blades that also dapple the grass
those that shine up as deeply green
from the female complexity of liquefied graze

and what excites his interest most
also makes the girls who see him
giggle behind their hands
hiding their glee in a fan of fingers
finding in this a fascinated shock of common earth
for perhaps they are thinking 'it cannot be thus for us'

and the boys run
laughing along the fence
in a stir and swirl
of shadow their youth touching through
where they stop and grip the wire almost climbing
to take a happy glance
through the tessellated shade of the link and chain
leaving such a lovely and delicate darkness
well beyond their reach

... if we worry about love, why not war

imagine my uncle
his intended beloved
blown to a ghost
in the blitz
her body seeding the blasted streets
life lost in crimson rubble
her spirit rising like brick dust
smouldering up and out
from the ruination of a building's romance
suddenly deaf to the sound
of sirens
and the otherwise
forgotten horrors
of these deadly heavens
the Luftwaffe heartless
and heroic
like a locust storm
thick with lost angels
sawing the crop of a doomed generation
their bomb doors
shitting death on the city
and though she was a simple
flesh-and-blood woman
photographed in a nurse's rank
she surrendered herself
to the mournful memory of grieving
as it is
with each light
we take to the grave
that luminous fire still glowing in ash
those lips
like roses in gauze
that name
on a whispering stone
two hearts for the earth
one to bury
one to carry away

Stone Horses

as man is but a mammal so am I
and more than I would dare admit
I've much in common
with the snuffling bull
who worships
at the vulva of the heifer in first heat
I've seen his helpless nostrils flared to breathe
inhaling her wet pheromones
he snorts an estrus invitation
drawn from deep within her menstruating womb
then tests the amber flavour of her gush
to lick the salty liquors of desire
much like a bitter word he longs to speak
he celebrates those pungent waters
flooding his bull mind
bellowing forth with the heady vapors of exhilarating froth
as with a deep exhaustion he exhales
and snorts as great whales snort
taking in and expelling the sea
before he dives in darkness fathoms deep

Darling, may I touch your pinkletink

in those early years of marriage
when we walked the back lane
forming the long island of meander
leading through the spring swale
surrounding us behind the house
where thimbleberries ripened through the fence
pressing crushed areolas of small fruit brambled
on the full bosom of the wet fields of Somerset
and as we strolled we heard
from both before and aft
the thrilled chorus of the swamp
singing among the red branches
of dogwood piercing the stillness
both lace and leaf
like the life of the heart throbbing
through a green mirror of algae
and something comes true—so eventual
it might
winter in us
like blush on the cheek
coming in from the cold

and I am remembered of
the quick black pollywog
pulsing in a jar
in the dill-coloured water
we stole from the pond
at school
and what it was it also seemed
flooding the world
in verdant release after my son's epithalamium
watching a swan's breast
advancing through High Park
its white reflection chasing feather-form
within the gentle chevron
of a wave's result

that proof of going towards forever
as it is with
where the hand goes
plunging in to release the stopper
in a warm bath
for the soapy clock-wind whirling
to a lovely gurgle in the gullet of a thirsty drain

we were the especial silence
at the centre
of all that singing
and it mattered not
how quietly we went

there was this secret knowledge
even of our shadow presence
even of the lucid darkness
within the limpid veil
of the least movement of the light
we were overheard by the grey caress
of bullfrogs listening
as though
to be caught singing were a sin
as the farm dog Tip
asleep in the cool
dip of the earth in the forsythia shade
of the veranda remains in the mind
long after he's under the grass
and I'm crooning on the porch
full voiced and unembarrassed
when my uncle says
"what the hell
are you doing …"

and I know it's not a question
but an accusation

Peeling Burn

why is it that long ago
when we were young lovers
you took such pleasure
peeling the sun-crimson skin
from my shoulders
which were three-days fragrant
with vinegar and aloe
and aging in the cool sting
of soothing medication
as I felt
the intimate draw and pluck
of your nails
catching the thin translucent
tarnish of lost epidermis
that came away in satisfying shivers
like papery sheets of dried veneer
a kind of shed lacquer
as though I were wood stained
in hot weather
refurbished to the raw grain
of original oak

leave me then
to those blushing maps
those red islands
with flesh-coloured shores
where the heart might startle
and take to the air
like a blue song in the fluttering pulse of summer

The Leaf of Eve Becoming the World

in the nineteen fifties
fashionable women's swimsuits
sported what were called *modesty panels*
short rayon skirts
that bloomed with wading
like water lilies
floating in still lagoons
those black-as-oil ponds of the orient
the perfectly doubled sky
shining on the surface
with the unacknowledged vanity of heaven
what the mind sees
imagining the silken blue interior
of a closed up jewelry box
and where the hips vanish
sheltered by drift
step deep and then step deeper in
there below the discontinuation of light
a liquefaction of darkness
caressing the skin
and the hands outstretched
as in surrender
the body becomes the world

In the Midst of Sweet Confusion

if I think of my love
in the midst
of her sweet confusion
with me there in the seed purse
of her body and mind
as though I am life in the soaked
and muddy rain-rich earths of May
perhaps I'll seep away
into such a shining darkness
like the warmed-through light in the chapel
from the work of a glazier's hand
or the sun on a pool
of morning going deep as light goes
when it carries the green burden of shade
oh we are God's darlings then
in the hide-and-seek gardens
shaping ourselves
in the secretive palm-shadows of Eden
under heaven's umbilicus moon
that is white in the blue of the day
like the milk stain
a new mother might weep
at the hungering voice of her child
oh we are such natural creatures
with a gift from unwrapping the heart
and to think
of the swelling of apples
the blush of a ripening bough
when we're pink at the throat
like a fever of flame you might glimpse
as the proof of the soul
with a lock and a key made from starlight
and a door in the earth for the rose

**... on finding a volume called
"The Female Orgasm" in amongst
used books set out on a long table
at a rummage sale in the vestry of
Grace Anglican Church
in Port Dover etc. ...**

there it sits among the well-thumbed
much-read paperback copies
of bodice rippers   murder mysteries and titles by
Thoreau, Dickens, Hemingway
a few local vanities
moldering Latin readers
black-and-gold jacketed school atlases
and old water-damaged
pencil-bothered books
mostly from the time
when young boys wore knickerbockers
and thought about war
with girls clad in hemmed gingham
let out to the knee
and mother-made blouses
pearling with unmatched buttons
stray threads and broad stitches
in blue knots
that come loose at the heart

and I lift it out by the covers
like I'm plucking a hen
and hold up the mischief
to the mortified attention
of the woman
who is making the sale
"a full bag for two dollars"
she chirps
as I show her the title
suggesting I might buy it
just to say
I found a book called *The Female Orgasm*
at the rummage sale in her church
and I crack the endpaper
revealing that it is a text book
a scholarly treatise for psychology majors
a well-researched clinical study
on the medical
and psychologically natural benefits of sexual climax
and she blushes as the woman beside me jokes
"It's too late for me" …

The Stone Woman

"... after being taken captive, Huascar's cap was filled with llama piss, (and) his natural desire was mocked by putting him to bed with a long stone dressed up as a woman ...(on the instruction from his brother Atahualpa, captive emperor of the Incas) Inca soldiers murdered Huascar and tossed his body in the river ..."
The Last Days of the Incas
Kim MacGuire

"... and it came to pass, when they were in the field, that Cain rose up against Abel his brother, and slew him."
Genesis 4, viii

the Spanish prize emperor Atahualpa
from captivity
ordered the death of his brother Huascar
pretender to the throne of the Incas
long after Atahualpa
had murdered all his brother's
wives and children
assassinating and torturing
most every member of his fraternal family
Atahualpa—choked by Spanish garrote
at the command of his captor
governor Pizarro, general Pizarro
weeping Pizarro—and then
Atahualpa's body burned
in its royal clothing
burned like a saint, burned
like the corpse of Hitler
sneering through flame
at the Reichstag, immolated
like a Buddhist monk
photographed in American occupied Saigon
or the unburnable heart of the poet
Percy Bysshe Shelley
lying in a bed of fire
on a sandy beach in Italy
before all that
like the second child

in the womb of Eve
the first fratricidal farmer
Cain— inquiring of God
"am I my brother's keeper?"

the suffering Huascar

was made to sleep
with a long stone
dressed as a woman
to mock his natural desire

and if God might hear
the blood
that crieth out of the earth

and we might dream a dream
of ourselves as vulva crowned
children of Adam
sons tethered to the deep
and uterine beauty
of the flesh-warm cave of water and bone
floating like astronauts in space
concerned by mother-ship starlight
seen through lovely darkness
in the primal bleary glimpse
and breviary breath of light
like an almost drowned
and drowning still
incarnation of individual life
gasping for air
and born to fear
like all pretenders to the throne of life
as though we ourselves
were not always
and forever
pretending toward the light
like smoke rising from masks of fire

Victorious Virgin

The Victorious Virgin was the name that accompanied the nose art on a WWII Halifax bomber made famous by Canada's notorious practitioner of nose art Matthew Ferguson. The rebuilt Halifax sits in the aviation museum in Trenton where the nose art was visible for only one day before it was ordered painted over as being thought to be 'politically incorrect' and potentially offensive to visitors.

looking up
from the museum floor
at the Halifax bomber
looming as a long-shadowed machine of war
we see
in slight relief
like writing on an antique coin
the painted-over letters
ghosting out from shining brown
shimmering in the light like watered silk
I glimpse the low relief of something
from the bellum past
some lover's name
perhaps — I wonder as I guess at
V i r g i n i a — spelling slow
as finger-follow in a child
when Mr. Flower
volunteers the truth
with wry smile sharing
it's *Victorious Virgin*
and I know
nose art
recall having seen the buxom
Vargas girls and movie stars — the hot list
of babes — Betty Grable
Veronica Lake, the zaftig Jane Russell
all scantily clad *it* girls from the forties
these being the reason
those red-blooded boys
risked all — to make it home

to make that old connection between flesh and night
blonde bombshells dropping down
with come-hither hips and open thighs

the sort of women
who might break a boy in two
or crush his heart beneath a crimson shoe
and they
were mostly boys
those men
you see them smiling
as they climbed aboard to take
the swivel seat
within the bubbled glass
behind the threatening poke of guns

you'll see their names out in the yard
in lamentation
on the walls, the names
a chisel whispers to the stone a sound
good friends might weep to hear
a sister kneels to set a flower in a neck of glass
a student rubs her pencil's edge
to mark a stranger's disconnected grief
and in this graphite sob
she sees a classmate touch his gilded wing

officiousness dictates
'efface the sexy girl' … she might offend
the sensitive … as someone shouts
come here and see this nearly absent gun
it rusts away like plumbing left to time

   … imagine how those bullets sang – whew!
      they tore those valiant men in half

Old Age

Make That My Metaphor

I am all
for involvement with spring-smooth things
see how there the closed up lily
split along its calyx
like a green and pursy seam of life
make that my metaphor
take in the apple being born inside the aromatic bud
caress the silken petal
of the delicate rose relaxing open in the sun
and when the sliding hither garden snail
liquefies the waking earth
to leave its shining trail
it seems much like slow desire on the inner thigh
come to include important beauties
of the body and its mucus-polished flesh
consider how the painted goddess
on her throne reveals her softening to show
her nether shell presenting like a silent kiss
bestowed in fragrant surrender
to the waves that love her well
oh she becomes like any other all-revealing creature
of this universal sea

Were I

were I to meet you
in your plastic shoes
and you me
in my cowboy boots
when we were both
small in the rain
lost among all that it meant
to be
casting short shadows
with new minds
when our mothers were young
and our fathers
were shaving their dreams
in the soap scent
of long-ago morning
rinsing their razors in time before time
would we have
loved the other
me in my worn-down heels
the sugar-foot lad
and you
the princess with painted toes
shining up from the floor
like chips of broken glass

oh we were playing at promise
I on my cockhorse
in the orchard
on the farm
my hat a ten-gallon green
and you in your pinafore
undressing and dressing your dolls
like the come and go
of the sea
to a darkening stone that lies
high on the shale of the shore

when you were a girl
your umbilical beautiful ultra white tummy
with its feminine lip and rim
like a green pomegranate
impossibly perfect with seed
desire abiding in sunlit
mirrors of the ribbon-watered moon
and I a boy
with my whip-tailed
star-dazzled want
like ghost galaxies
glazing the milk spill of night
the voluminous smear at the swirling edge
of mammalian chaos

what's cervical mucus of the spirit
what's ovum-mystical life

you in the city and
I on the farm
we awaited love's knowledge unborn

The Light that Sees Us

I am not alone
in the multi-mirrored room
lifting a final set of free weights for the morning
doing curls and then
flexing my limbs in straight-arm flight
like the wing beats
of a human bird
my body unwillingly reflected in silver
flashes of artificial light
meanwhile
in the strange intimacy
of the gymnatorium
a young woman
lying on the floor
engages in a rapid series
of pelvic thrusts
breathing harder with each
subsequent exertion as though
she were responding to the illusory
movements of a phantom lover
and I am not the last bad angel
betrayed by the beautiful energy of a blue sky
I am not Icarus
my wet feathers gummed in warm wax
falling to the floor
through the dark melt of a sun-drenched sea, no
I'm simply an old man
standing with
the marionette of my will

strung to the muscled machinery
of my bones
and so I carry on
until, setting the twelve-pound bells
back in their cradle
with a soft and unavoidable clang
I make my exit
doing my very best
to seem like the silent departure
of a careful father
to the young woman
breathing heavily, her eyes closed in concentration
as it is with each of us
when we hold
our individual and otherwise invisible darkness
as though it were enough
to make the light that sees us disappear

In the Muddy Bed of Creation

we were speaking yesterday
my elder cousin and I
of fifty years ago
when one female member of our clan
shocked the family
by coming to the annual picnic
and donning a bikini
for the summer swim
in the blue-water river
across the road from our great-uncle's house in Mooretown

what did her grandfather
make of the shameful showing of flesh
her bronzing umbilicus newly revealed
like a button pulled in too tight by a thread
he being
a dour and mostly unsmiling
man of the cloth
and what did her grandmother
make of it all, she being the vicar's wife
behind whom
we walked in a gaggle
crossing the street
and going unshod and ginger foot
over hot tar and sharp gravel
to the dock ladder
some leaping into the flow
and some wading rung-by-rung slow

we'd followed our great-aunt there
like waterfowl imprinted upon
her ultra-white body
her elderly thighs gone blue in the vein

this is what time
will do
it will make you wonder
about who you were
when you were young
with your toes sunk to the nail
in the muddy bed of creation

Bewilderment of the Heart

*"The Lord will smite you with madness and blindness
and with bewilderment of the heart."
Deuteronomy 28:28*

I was chasing a bag in the wind
when it had settled down
on a patch of road
as it came to rest out of reach
with a seemingly slow resolve to elude me
like the shadow of a thoughtful man
I'm bending down to touch
the stain of my body
like a wet splash thinning as it dries
to an almost grey translucent lessening of light
as though it were only the dream lens of a close-at-hand mirage
affecting ephemeral darkness
pebbled through with macadam and grit

and I felt the tar force of a cantilevered rising and falling
like waves within water
feeling what breaks both ways
inward and outward
erupting and cascading   rising and plunging
lifting out   and settling down
to a reconfiguring swell
within the amplitude of an energetic pause

though I laugh now at the occasion tantalized by desire
for the bag I pursued in the wind
set sail and remained out of reach
just as I arrived it lit and then scurried away
as though it thought I were a child
in pursuit of ever-elusive wonder
instead of being an increasingly angry
old man chasing a bag in the wind

Open

open your eyes, open your heart
open your mind, open your arms
open your thighs, open your infolding flesh
involve me there
within that flowering
as though you were a butterfly in gauze
a garden in the sun
or loamy earth
beneath the muddy fragrance of the rain
and I will enter
blue rivers of desire
life pulsing round each thirsting root
one season lived in solitude
three seasons   lived alone

I am content to be contained
like pebbles plunging in the circular rhythms
of a radiant pool within the secret sorrows
of your solitary soul

My Love is Like an All-Day Rain

my love is like an all-day rain
that seeps into the earth
and greens the lawn
then soaks the humus in the root
to feel the world in growth
it pools on paths
and beads on branches
jeweled with shining tears of light
the upturned leaf
in thirst will drink the welling sky
and dampened colours
darken as they blush
in deeper shades
as though from phantom hearts
and quickened pulses
of reciprocated liquid touch
the trace lines
of a rivulet on glass
become a clear caress
meandering in aqueous response
to an overburdening descent
see where water enters
at these healing seams of clay
how close that voice
to whispering
insentient alluvium alive with seed
the fracturing creation
of fecundities of loam

the ditches swell
and streams come cooler to the lake
from where they've met
in cloud-sourced hills
to where they lose their names
I know the night will come
as invitation to tomorrow's sun
bring on blue heaven
and her vanquished stars
her ever-present often
absent moon
but keep this rain in mind, my love
these ethers gauzed in grey
were once the amorous continuum of weather
caught within the petals of your crimson rose

A Tourist in Bath Considers Lovers from the Past

we were walking the walls
above the Roman baths
which were dry stone - evaporate rock
soaked in time-softened shapes of permanent thirst
like the ghost rivers
of a rainless valley

on the same day
we visited the vacant rooms
where Jane Austen wintered
and if I thought of her
I thought also
of ink on glass
in the black wells of school
lifting my nib
with its darkened tear
its fragrance of oakmoss
and the indigo-blue trail
of words left behind
by the slow thinker's
mind-tangled hand

and if I might imagine
the mineral pools
of the past
with naked gentry
lowering themselves
into the liquid heat
and then the lingering there
of an aqueous intimacy
where the soul and the spirit
meet and float
like the drifting

of veils in breath
what caresses the flesh
the body feels in the blood and bone
as it is with the rocking of waves
or the moon motion of rising tides

and for all the tourists
in the city
take this beautiful caution of the heart
concerning the handsome remainder
and the lovely residue of statuary dust

wherever the shadow falls
it is not there but for the sun

and in seeking the cool of the shade
we vanish

Ode to the Lake as Lover

*"... the wave that died the death which lovers love
living in what it sought; as if this spasm
had not yet passed ..."*
      Percy Bysshe Shelley, "The Boat on the Serchio"

sometimes I see
the lake that is become your lover
when you walk towards
the yearning deep surrendering
within each intimate swell
that crests upon your beautiful body
the tip of each wave
curling under where it rises falling
away in a wash along the shining flesh
to touch all colour with a darkening hue
as though in sacred ablution
to break with liquid blue
in its dance of desire its little dance of death
seeking the sacramental font
of all creation
in that silkening cleft
and I wonder what it is you feel
there in those inconstant fathoms
of mutual response
where water laps
its tongue in tantalizing thirst
how you shiver then
and rise upon your toes
your arms like angel wings that glide at rest in flight
as you stagger within the energy of that exchange
receiving life in mutable light upon the lake
your image pooling as though in prisms of oil
that shimmer and vanish and shatter
as you move within the swooning
swirl of nature's cool caress
to feel the shuddering of a coupling presence unopposed
a cosmic tenderness comingling
with the sweet commotion diving in
where minnows school and are the soul of things
though felt remain unseen

When Love is Like Knocking the Clay from the Plough

in the silage
and on the hay
in the fragrance of
rolled oats and molasses
and as it is
with the sweet odour
of cut grass and cow flap still green
or the high pong
of hog chop or how
wheat straw smells of mid-summer sunlight
softening the mow
or dust in the bean row
with dirt choking the light
as it dims with the tilth of the day
turning the earth
on the spring tooth and the harrow
or under the giant drum
of the roller
a rock-rattle watched for leveling
so the wind-wild soil
will settle upon the sewn seed
all these and a closing in of white
on the bird-limed stone
oat chaff and marrow
and swine spoor
flung at the root and draping the fences
in timothy strings
dripping the redolent rags of manure
a dark wake
a wide swath
a visceral moment of darkness comes shallow
in shades like shadows in trees
that follow the man in the field
first catching blue air
and then falling

transforming the mutable glebe
with fertile aromas
ammonium rich and ...
reminding how love is
like knocking the clay from the plough
or what
flies from the tread of the wheel
when the tractor comes home in the dark

whenever I feel
the heart in the heat of a thigh
next to mine
or a palm warm as a pulse
on the back of my hand
I am there in the youth
of first things
made memory deep
as the full boat
rides deep and so deeper for that
in the come-to-me cresting of waves

2020 winning poem in
ACM Poetry Contest
(Angela Consolo Mankiewicz)

On Saying Farewell to a Mattress

we've lost the mattress
that took the shape of our bodies
like water beneath a buoyant boat
the still curve of the bone of the hip
like the gentle caressing of the keel
see there the age-old history of sleep
surrendered in timeless dimensions
the pillow-top ticking of marriage at rest
in calm waves
that are motionless dips
like evaporate puddles
in the warming away of late-summer rain
this evident dreaming
snow-angels that carry the body
and hold the heart in full darkness
like the floating through branches of moonlight
caressing the earth like a veil
how we love makers codify memory
like the sheets of a ship in the wind
how the future comes ancient before us
in the days that we rest
in the shade
here one man's long hollow's remembered
and a woman's
a shallow recalled
take the tearstain of stars in the evening
that fall dry
in the weeping of night
while the shape in the mirror
I'm holding
is lost in the absence of light

Unseen

what stops at the door
of the bedroom at night
where dreamers
are keeping their secrets
in sleep
with the wind at the casement
and the moon
in the glass
I've a mind
for the movement
of limbs in the air
like breath in the willow
that's stirring its nest
or the song
of the evening that sings
in the eaves
how the owl's on the barn hip
his ear
to the earth
or the emerald of knowledge
that blinks in the hay
what the water's reflecting
when no one is there
in the luminous absence
of depth in a wave
the body has faith
that the morning will come
while the heart
in its bone-hold goes slow
with an ear
to the doorframe
and an eye like a key
for shaping the darkness

with gossamer light
see there
how the lovers
slip into the mist
like Juliet dying
or Eve at the gate
we might cover the distance
unseen by the seeing of things that aren't real

Syntribating Sweetheart

even now this late in life
I think of sex all day

and as I do *sometimes* I think of us
when we were young
and dangerous in love
late adolescent amorous and mother warned
and only just beginning to learn
the meaning of each other's *genderness*

and as I remember you
in your short skirt
the pleated blue-green Campbell plaid
held closed with a kilt pin
that seemed to me
the silver hasp of paradise
I dreamed of how it might
be winter cool
upon your thighs

and you my syntribating sweetheart
nervously kicking your half-loose loafer
as you studied
in your farouche and almost falling socks

our life in truth pursuant
to the rub and tickle of a momentary itch
knowing how to hold at bay
a stupid urgency that ruins all and everything
like frost that burns the living leaf

we were distracted by the need to memorize
the meaning of my Shelley
and you your Sigmund Freud

A Bed Too Big for Both of Us

the night we wed
two youths ago, three years
since when we'd met to think upon
the past with dime-glass draft
set out for service in a dozen empty foams
the bottom dregs circumferenced in salt
the rims
like bells of brassy instruments
angelic silence in the smoky light
and slaked by shining thirsts in dimming air
we hardly talked at all
for I was shy
and barely off the farm
meanwhile your body woman warm
you sat upon my lap
with me your faux intended beau
we kissed but once
and strangely said farewell to solitude

and now
four decades hence
some sixteen thousand nights
and more
we seek each loving slumber
in familiar arms
within a bed
too big for both of us
and yet too small for one
the many changes
rounding out the crowd of selves
the boy, the youth, the man, the husband
father, friend and
you, the girl, the woman

wife and mother
all the separated souls
in us are shaped in seven-bodied foolishness
by passing time
the heart count slow to wake
yet quick to sleep

imagine dreaming
while the knowing tree
regathers all its flavours
to a single pluck
unfallen from the heavy bough
the naked innocence
reforming round its sheltered seed
oh then how life
refigures in the fuse
the bud believes in autumn
as the winter keeps its faith in spring
go hide your common shame
and sorrows in the shade

the light will have
its shadow in the leaf
and the wind will make the darkness wild

Swept Away

thoughts framed in a poem after reading
D. H. Lawrence's poem "Sex Isn't Sin" a glosa

… Know yourself, O know yourself, that you are mortal

sometimes I think of you abed my love
alone with all it means
to have your private pleasures proved
and basking in the valediction
of a solitary kindness to the self
to lift the musky fragrance
of a quiet sea in swells between the thighs
to touch your redolent vulva deep within
and dampened
as by desire liquefied
the labial vermilion blushed
like fulling petals of a rain-struck rose
crossed by both light and shade and twinned with heat
your hand perfumed by ecstasy's arousal
wave on wave the consequential wake
a thrill subsiding in the rise and fall
of what the Chinese poets call
ten thousand rubs

and know
the sensitive delicacy of your sex, in its ebbing to and fro

the intimate and repetitious
fingertip and cuticle moon
caressing silk and polishing its pearl

and the mortal reserve of your sex

the quickening heart gone slow
the tender nipples ripening
and rising roseate and gorgeously engorged
lifting in the areola stain

orgasmic summering like berries blushing in the cane
and as you maritate and are become divine
you lift your yearning hips
and arch your supple spine
until the crying out
as though in agony
your fingers thrust within
that lovely fold
some call the *cunt*
a word envowelled by a lover's truth
a word that does not make me love you less
but more your body thus receives itself
and loved in nature
for its maiden-form perfection in design

a consummate voluptuous and sour sweet
enlivening of life to feel and feel
and feel again the fertile mucus
cresting in its velvet well of smoothest skin
like fruit-spoil in an over-ripened peach

O know yourself, O know your sex!

and by anatomy of gender
and the exaltation of your coming there
and having come you long to come again

know that it is both human and sublime
to be simply and completely
swept away …

* * *

Far Off in the Night Sky

i

in casual conversation
with Sunday-morning sunlight
pooling in the living room
like newly-pressed canola oil
spilled and shining up from the well-polished wood
of the narrow-board floor
we were talking in that glamour
of sexual obsession
as the zeitgeist of our times
how in the broad continuum of gender
though slow in the uptake we learn
of the wide range of concerns
of the body
as defined by desire and design
what might an old mind make
of completion and surrender
or of the nouns and verbs
we use in this regeneration of language
as though
there weren't always incandescent
blue-winged creatures
awaiting discovery in the dark regions
of an unnamed forest
hiding in the deeply mysterious
chiaroscuro of the remote wilderness
flexing their beauty
as they unfold in first flight
as all unknown imago
in metamorphosis
release their secret selves
from the chrysalis of their own making

ii

and so I say
how I learned of sex
not in school, not from my parents,
not from my friends, or cousins, but
by reading
Everything You Wanted to Know about Sex but Were Afraid to Ask
and the greatest surprise to me
was the revelation of the existence of the female orgasm

in reply
she confessed that she
did not know there was such a thing
until after she was married

iii

is that revelation sad
or naïve
or charming

I do not know

though deep
on the ocean floor

lingering in darkness
something moves
something we have never seen

If I Were So Compelled by Life

if I were so compelled by life
to clarify desire
it would by law of nature
and necessity
include the lovely fold of flesh
that rarely sees the sun
the silken maiden form
the body holds
in candle white and tinged in coral pink within
a roseate design concealed from light
and I've a Latin lexicon for that
a variorum of childhood words
a juvenile taxonomy
an old concordance of anatomy
stolen from forbidden breath
and tongue touched sounds we said aloud at school
in secret nooks

cold favour to the curious child in me
to think on darkness
in the adult world
the garden where we walk our secret thoughts in dream
where fingers drop
like drones upon the velvet petals of the summer rose

An Essay/Review by Vanessa Shields

John B Lee's *Darling May I Touch Your Pinkletink* is a poetic tour-de-force into one man's experience of sensual and sexual love through the vulva-red glasses of childhood, adolescence, youth and old age. This collection exemplifies Lee's romantic and devotional erotic voice as it entwines his sensual and sexual experiences of love with the wild steadiness of human sexual curiosities and discoveries. His childhood fascination with female genitalia –

> *"...the sweet cleft is gilded in pink*
> *and ruffled within by labial silk and most intimate satins*
> *set with the pip of its clitoral pearl*
> *vermillion and pink and choral colour*
> *scented by the fragrance*
> *of vaginal flora and musky micturate..."*
>   (*from 'Proud'*)

extends into a life-long devotion to honouring, admiring and giving pleasure to the female body. Love is a powerful theme as well. Through Lee's sharing of his sexual desires, dreams, pleasures and confusions, we witness the character arc from sweet, farmboy innocence and giddy teen playfulness to the blooming of a sexually aware man who pays attention to the needs and wants of the physical body as it dives into the deeps of love.

As a poet, Lee's gift for the erotic is as ripe as the fruit he uses to describe the tastes of the vulva. There is a clear vein of worship to these fine female parts throughout the collection. If you're wondering what it looks like hidden or spread wide, how it feels pressed by finger or tongue, what it tastes and smells like, Lee's sensual descriptions will leave you panting to make your own discoveries.

He is no slouch when it comes to seeping metaphor into every fold of the explicit stories he tells. The red lipstick of the 'old, well-meaning' ladies from his childhood remains an important stain on his poetic cheek. Perhaps the farmland animal fornication too continues to build his tower of tellings about sexuality in his poems. Lee is a horny bull who *"even now this late in life I think of sex all day"* – is a strong contender in the world of erotic poetry.

The most beautiful poem in the collection, 'When Love Is Like Knocking the Clay from the Plough', gathers Lee's past, present and future into a stunning metaphorical homage to the land, to the purity of 'first things', to the devastating ability to reflect on the self as a lover – one who is able to love, to be loved, and to express this love through pleasure....even when in old age pleasure might only be felt through the heat of words in an erotic poem.

Vanessa Shields,
poet, author of 'I Am That Woman',
'Look At Her', and
'thimbles' (forthcoming spring 2021)

Author Biographical Note:

In 2005 John B. Lee was inducted as Poet Laureate of Brantford in perpetuity. The same year he received the distinction of being named Honourary Life Member of The Canadian Poetry Association and The Ontario Poetry Society. In 2007 he was made a member of the Chancellor's Circle of the President's Club of McMaster University and named first recipient of the Souwesto Award for his contribution to literature in his home region of southwestern Ontario and he was named winner of the inaugural Black Moss Press *Souwesto Award* for his contribution to the ethos of writing in Southwestern Ontario. In 2011 he was appointed Poet Laureate of Norfolk County (2011-14) and 2020 he was appointed the Poet Laureate of the CCLA Canada Cuba Literary Alliance. In 2015 Honourary Poet Laureate of Norfolk County for life and in 2017 he received a Canada 150 Medal from the Federal Government of Canada for "his outstanding contribution to literary development both at home and abroad." A recipient of over eighty prestigious international awards for his writing he is winner of the $10,000 CBC Literary Award for Poetry, the only two time recipient of the People's Poetry Award, and 2006 winner of the inaugural Souwesto Orison Writing Award (University of Windsor). In 2007 he was named winner of the Winston Collins Award for Best Canadian Poem, an award he won again in 2012. He has well-over seventy books published to date and is the editor of seven anthologies including two best-selling works: *That Sign of Perfection*: poems and stories on the game of hockey; and *Smaller Than God*: words of spiritual longing. He co-edited a special issue of *Windsor Review—Alice Munro: A Souwesto Celebration* published in the fall of 2014. His work has appeared internationally in over 500 publications, and has been translated into French, Spanish, Korean and Chinese. He has read his work in nations all over the world including South Africa, France, Korea, Cuba, Canada and the United States. He has received letters of praise from Nelson Mandela, Desmond Tutu, Australian Poet, Les Murray, and Senator Romeo Dallaire. Called "the greatest living poet in English," by poet George Whipple, he lives in Port Dover, Ontario where he works as a full time author.

www.ingramcontent.com/pod-product-compliance
Lightning Source LLC
Chambersburg PA
CBHW020536080526
44583CB00013B/884